Praise for *My Father's Business*

Eddie Jones has crafted the kind of timely inspirational stories that encourage the timid, humble the proud, and remind us that God really wants to use our gifts and talents.

> ~ Ray Blackston, author of *Flabbergasted,*
> *Lost in Rooville, A Delirious Summer, The Trial of*
> *Alex Lord, Par for the Course, Last Mango*
> *in Texas,* and *A Pagan's Nightmare.*

There is something about the power of a story well told that inspires and sticks with you. This book is so refreshing because I learned things about Walt Disney, Mother Teresa, and General George Patton that I'd not heard previously. Author Eddie Jones hits home on inspiring us through the power of story. Great read—and lots of room for personal notes, too.

> ~ C. Hope Flinchbaugh, author of
> *I'll Cross the River, Out of North Korea,*
> *Spiritually Parenting Your Preschooler,*
> and *Across the China Sky.*

Love it. Easy to read, poignant, common sense approach and scripturally sound. Sure to challenge and reassure simultaneously. Great way to start your morning!

> ~ L.W. Rondeau, author of *The Other Side of Darkness*
> (2012 Selah Award for best new novel), *America II: The*
> *Reformation,* and *It Really Is a Wonderful Life.*

This is not a sit-on-the-shelf devotional book. Indeed, readers will find Eddie Jones intriguing stories, wise quotes, and pertinent questions helpful as they learn to discern and do God's will. This small book offers huge impact handing readers hope, provoking thoughtful reflection, and encouraging life-changing application.

~ Arlene Knickerbocker, owner of *The Write Spot,*
and author of *Open the Door to Another Realm,*
a Poetic Journey of Devotion.

Yes, it is a 30-day devotional, but so much more! Whether you are an executive seeking solutions to today's world, or a home school Mom who needs encouragement to continue on the path you feel is right for your family, this is a must read! It will transform your mind from the world's way of life to what God, our Father, intended all along: to know His will, and be doing it.

~ "Simply" Sue Falcone, author of
The Lighthouse of Hope:
A Day by Day Journey to Fear Free.

With a blend of Scriptures, history and storytelling, Eddie Jones invites the reader to engage in thirty attitude changing vignettes by journaling. Thoughtful. Soul searching. Compelling.

~ Cleo Lampos, author of
Teaching Diamonds in the Tough:
Mining the Potential in Every Child.

Even though I've been a Christian for fifty years, Eddie Jones' devotional book, *My Father's Business,* couldn't speak more clearly to my spiritual needs if he'd written it just for me. Not only does Eddie base each devotional on an appropriate Scripture and give a related quote from Oswald Chambers, he uses a brief, thought-provoking anecdote to draw our attention to the main point of each devotional. Each chapter has a "Discern" page for the student to record his own observations and a "Do" page that might appropriately be labeled as a "To Do" page. Viewing this book as "just another devotional book" would be a huge mistake. It's far more valuable.

~ Roger Bruner, author of
Found in Translation,
Lost in Dreams and *I Started a Joke.*

About to Bury Your Dreams at Sea? Read This First! In a time when Christians have succumbed to the world's way of pursuing dreams, (build a bigger platform, hire better publicity and hijack your children's college funds), *My Father's Business* lassos the reader and redirects him back to the Director of our Dreams. Each selection has scripture, and two daily questions to prompt the reader to action with Jones reminding us, "God often begins with menial assignments, tiny tithes and insignificant gestures." With witty titles like "Work at Bigger King" (Commitment), Roast Yourself (Humility), and Send Scraps (Persistence), the author exhorts the dreamless and discouraged to retrieve their God-inspired dreams.

~ Carol G. Stratton,
author of *Changing Zip Codes:*
Finding Community Wherever You're Transplanted.

I highly recommend *My Father's Business* by Eddie Jones for anyone who truly desires God's will in his/her life. For me, the past two years have been ones of major changes. Reading this book confirmed and affirmed much of where I believe God is leading. I especially love the opportunities to journal (Discern and Do) at the end of each reading.

~ Marjorie Vawter
Freelance Editor and Writer

My Father's Business takes the reader on a clever journey of inspiration that begins with faith, is strengthened by vision, sculpted by humility and sealed with commitment. The chapters are short, to the point, and ooze with inspiration. Each chapter builds upon the previous, so that before realizing it, the reader begins walking in preparation to do the unthinkable for God.

Nan Trammell Jones, author of the devotional blog, *Morning Glory* at Jubilant Light Ministries at www.jubilantlight.com.

MY FATHER'S BUSINESS

30 Inspirational Stories for Discerning and Doing God's Will

My Father's Business:
A 30 Day Daily Devotional for Seeking and Doing God's Will

ISBN: 978-1-64526-925-0
Copyright © 2024
Cover Design by Wisdom House Book wisdomhousebooks.com
Book Design by Anna O'Brien: www.behindthegift.com

Available in print from your local bookstore, online, or from the publisher at: www.lighthousepublishingofthecarolinas.com

Library of Congress Cataloging-in-Publication Data
Jones, Eddie, 1957-
My Father's Business: 30 Inspirational Stories for Discerning and Doing God's Will /.— 2nd ed.

Printed in the United States of America

Table of Contents

The only reliable way to be truly guided by God is to assimilate the Word of God to your character. . . . Scripture reveals God's will only if we allow His Holy Spirit to apply it to our circumstances.

Oswald Chambers

Introduction

What does it mean to discern God's will for your life? How can you hear His call? The word *discernment* comes from two Latin words: *discernere* (to perceive) and *discretis* (to separate). To discern God's voice and will is to converse with Him. In both Hebrew and Greek, the word *will* means "to yearn." When we say, "Lord, Your will be done," we are asking God to infuse His deepest yearnings into our spirit and alter the circumstances of our lives in order that we may grow. God sees beyond our past and knows our secret desires, even those desires yet to be born. "In the same way, the Spirit helps us in our weakness. We do not know what we ought to pray for, but the Spirit himself intercedes for us with groans that words cannot express" (Romans 8:26, NIV).

As you seek to discern and do God's will, ask the following questions:

- Will this course of action use my gifts, talents, and passions?
- How has my previous experience prepared me for this task?
- Will this new opportunity cause me to be more loving?

- Is this an expansion of my influence for God?
- Will I feel more fulfilled and have a greater sense of inner peace?
- Who will benefit from my actions?
- What will it cost me and my family?
- Is this a time-sensitive opportunity?

We often complicate the business of knowing God's will, but His word is clear: "And You will seek Me and find Me, when you search for Me with all your heart" (Jeremiah 29:13 NKJV). Those who seek and ask, hear His voice. The following devotional stories illustrate how others have heard God's call and heeded His voice. My prayer is that you, too, will learn to recognize God's voice so that you will be able both to discern and to do His will.

Prayer does not fit us for the greater works; prayer <u>is</u> the greater work.

Oswald Chambers

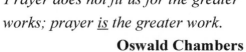

With Prayer, We Cannot Fail
(Piety)

And pray in the Spirit on all occasions with all
kinds of prayers and requests. With this in mind,
be alert and always keep on praying for all the
[Lord's people]. **Ephesians 6:18 (NIV)**

"Chaplain, sit for a moment. I want to talk to you about this business of prayer." George S. Patton stood by the window watching the steady rain. For days the Third Army had been bogged down due to the weather. "Chaplain," asked Patton, "How much praying is being done in the Third Army?" The Chaplain admitted that lately, not much.

"Chaplain, I am a strong believer in prayer. There are three ways that men get what they want: by planning, by working, and by praying. Any great military operation takes careful planning or thinking. Then you must have well-trained troops to carry it out: that's working. But between the plan and the operation there is always an unknown. That unknown spells defeat or victory, success or failure. Up to now, God has been very good to us. We have never retreated; we have suffered no defeats, no famine, no epidemics. This is because a lot of people back home are praying for us. We were lucky in Africa, in Sicily, and in Italy. Simply because people prayed. But we have to pray for ourselves too. We must ask God to stop these rains. This Army needs the assurance and the faith that God is with us. With prayer, we cannot fail."*

But *what if* we are forbidden to pray for the protection of our nation, the wisdom of our leaders, and the freedoms of our people? On August 29, 2011, a three-judge panel of the Fourth U.S. Circuit Court of Appeals ruled officials could not pray before public meetings. The ruling, in the case of Joyner v. Forsyth County, admonished public officials to refrain from invoking the name of Jesus.

To pray is to call upon God and to invite Him into conversation. The Greek word *enteuxis* is often translated "intercession." In the New Testament the word is used to describe a petition presented to a king on the behalf of another. A petition is not an unspoken request but a bold supplication that carries with it the signatures of those who dared to come before the ruling authorities. God listens to our silent prayers, but He also *longs* to hear our voices raised to the heavens, demanding justice for the oppressed and assistance for the wounded and hurting.

Between December 12 and December 14, 1944, two hundred and fifty thousand copies of General Patton's Prayer Card were distributed to the troops. On December 20, the rains ceased. For almost a week, American warplanes bombarded the German

---

*<http://www.pattonhq.com/prayer.html>

army that had been advancing under the cloak of fog. General Patton prayed for fair weather and God sent it.

Perhaps it's time to gather in our homes, churches, public squares, and courtrooms and ask God to have mercy on us and to forgive our sins. Each year the United States recognizes a national day of prayer. What our country needs is citizens who will pray without ceasing.

Will we embrace that challenge?

Discern: Read Nehemiah 1. What are the characteristics of Nehemiah's prayer? How did God answer Nehemiah's prayer in chapter 2?

_____

_____

_____

_____

_____

_____

_____

_____

Do: Make a prayer card. List at least ten prayer concerns—five for you, five for other people. Lift those requests up to the Lord every day. Expect answers.

_____

_____

_____

_____

_____

_____

_____

_____

_____

_____

_____

The thing that really testifies for God and for the people of God in the long run is steady perseverance, even when the work cannot be seen by others.

Oswald Chambers

Rubber Meets His Road
(Perseverance)

Therefore, my beloved brethren, be steadfast, immovable, always abounding in the work of the Lord, knowing that your labor is not in vain in the Lord. **1 Corinthians 15:58 (NKJV)**

When someone told Charles Goodyear that rubber from India could be used for a multitude of products, he spent years boiling rubber with magnesia, nitric acid, lime, and bronze powder trying to make it more useful. Every experiment failed. Depending upon the temperature, the natural properties of rubber made it too sticky, brittle, or pliable. But Goodyear continued to sink more money into his projects and his family into more debt.

Then in 1939, while standing beside a hot stove, Goodyear accidently brushed sulfur from his hands. As the rubber melted, it reacted with sulfur and produced vulcanized rubber, a flexible material that could be shaped into a variety of products. For months afterward if anyone asked where he might find Charles

Goodyear, he was told, "Look for the man without a penny in his pocket wearing an India-rubber cap, coat, shoes, and purse. That'll be Charles Goodyear."*

The Apostle Paul wrote to the struggling church in Corinth and encouraged its members to remain steadfast in their work within the Kingdom of God. To work in solitude, unnoticed by man, reveals our true character, motives, and passion. In the desert, away from the applause and at-a-boys, our "rubber meets His road."

If you *knew* you could succeed, what would you try to create, build, or write? Write it down in a journal. Pen it to a scrap of paper and keep it in your wallet. Look at your dream often.

Perseverance is more than blind faith and foolish determination. Perseverance is endurance combined with the absolute assurance that we will succeed. It is the quiet confidence that our course of action is correct—that our supreme effort and immovable determination will achieve for us the thing we seek.

Today Charles Goodyear's "accidental brush with luck" is everywhere, from the tires on our cars to hockey pucks on the ice.

The question is not, "Lord, will this work?"

The question is, "Will we?"

---

* adapted from *Speaker's Library of Business Stories, Anecdotes, and Humor* by Joe Griffith (Upper Saddle River, NJ: Prentice Hall, 1990).

Discern: Read 1 Corinthians 15:51-58. What motivation does Paul give the Corinthians for being steadfast in their work? Why should that also motivate us?

_____

_____

_____

_____

_____

_____

_____

_____

Do: What is your dream? Explore possibilities, investigate opportunities, and evaluate the risks and rewards. Write down your findings. Ask God to narrow your choices until His will is clear.

_____

_____

_____

_____

_____

_____

_____

_____

_____

_____

Love is the overflowing result of one person in true fellowship with another.
Oswald Chambers

Assemble Your Team
(Fellowship)

A cord of three strands is not quickly broken.
Ecclesiastes 4:12b (NIV)

Years ago an old man approached Dante Gabriel Rossetti, the famous 19th-century poet and artist and showed him some paintings. He asked, "What do you think, Mr. Rossetti?"

Rossetti studied them. After the first few, Rossetti knew the paintings were worthless; they did not display the least hint of artistic talent. Sensing Rossetti's disapproval, the old man apologized for wasting Rossetti's time and started toward the door. He'd only taken a few steps before he turned and asked if Rossetti would look at a second batch of paintings. Rossetti reluctantly agreed, but after inspecting the first few, Rossetti grew excited.

"These, now, these are good. This artist shows great potential. With enough encouragement, perseverance, and practice I expect he might enjoy a great future as a renowned painter." Observing the old man's pensive expression, Rossetti asked, "Whose are these? Your son's?"

"No," said the man. "They're mine from...forty years ago. If only I had heard such praise then. But instead, I became discouraged and quit."*

Like this old man, God knows our talent blossoms when our spirits are lifted through encouraging words, words uttered by those who share our passion for a project and see the potential in its completion.

God delights in dead ends and closed doors. He loves desperate people who fall into His arms, pleading for help. Often He sends help in the form of new friends that catch our vision or strangers who recognize our talent, complimenting us on our efforts without prompting.

When we set out on a new course, we need to surround ourselves with individuals who share our vision. Find supporters who see what is unseen and believe in what has not yet been found. These individuals become our team, our inner circle. They will guard our heart when difficulties arise. A cord of three strands is not easily broken. Knit friendships with quality yarn.

---

*<http://www.motivational-well-being.com/motivational-stories-9.html>

Discern: Read Luke 5:17-26. What did the paralytic's friends see that he did not see? What were their outstanding qualities?

_____

_____

_____

_____

_____

_____

_____

_____

Do: Who's on your team? Ask your team members to pray for you regularly, at least 3 times a week.

_____

_____

_____

_____

_____

_____

_____

_____

_____

_____

_____

_____

_____

When you cannot hear God, you will find that He has trusted you in the most intricate way possible—with absolute silence, not a silence of despair, but one of pleasure, because He saw that you could withstand an even bigger revelation.

Oswald Chambers

Labor Heartily As Unto the Lord (Productivity)

Don't waste your time on useless work, mere busywork, the barren pursuits of darkness. Expose these things for the sham they are. It's a scandal when people waste their lives on things they must do in the darkness where no one will see. Rip the cover off those frauds and see how attractive they look in the light of Christ. Wake up from your sleep, Climb out of your coffins; Christ will show you the light! So watch your step. Use your head. Make the most of every chance you get. These are desperate times! **Ephesians 5:11-16 (MSG)**

When did *work* become a four-letter word? When did God's first command become a burden? Perhaps it began when we exchanged God's gift of joy through employment for the fleeting security of career entitlement. As the resource officer waits for us to clear out our desk, we cry, "You can't do this to me! I've been here since...." God intended for work to be more than a means of provision, position, and posturing. When we labor "heartily as unto the Lord," it becomes an act of worship.

Are you burned-out by a dead-end job instead of filled with fire for a cause, a craft, or a ministry? Do you fear you've missed the chance to make a difference? Don't worry. Our God is the Lord of second and third chances. His eyes roam the earth seeking those who will open the door when He knocks. Will you respond to His banging?

Here are four ways to make the most of every chance we get:

Find a problem and fix it. Opportunities are often disguised as problems. These challenges force us to explore other options, examine the resources we have, and push on. When faced with a dead end, listen for God to say, "This way." A closed door is only a dead end when we don't follow the detour signs.

Move with urgency. Open doors do not remain open forever. New opportunities are time-sensitive. Ground floors become foundations for tall buildings, so seize the moment. Don't wait, ponder, and procrastinate. By the time you act, it may be too late. If the chance to do something different, untried, and frightening excites you, walk through that open doorway.

Expect resistance. Often we mistake hardships for God's disapproval when, in fact, the rocks, weeds, and ruts are just confirmation that we're plowing new territory. Paul wrote to the church in Corinth, "A great and effective door has opened to me and there are many adversaries" (1 Corinthians 16:9, NKJV). Paul did not write, "Things are falling apart around me; I must have misunderstood what God said." The fastest point of sail is when the wind is against and slightly ahead of the boat, not blowing from behind.

Face down your fears. Don't let fear of the unknown stop you from doing what excites you. Wake up. Climb out. Watch your step. Use your head. Make the most of every chance you get. Christ will light your way.

These are desperate times. The world needs pioneers who are willing to put aside the slothful acts of darkness and step boldly into the future. Today, if God is calling you to a new challenge, don't hesitate.

Discern: Read Genesis 30:25-31:13. Jacob was desperate. How did he make the most of his situation?

_____

_____

_____

_____

_____

_____

_____

_____

Do: Feeling desperate? Read Romans 8:26-39. Write down the promises God makes in those verses. Ask Him to confirm one of those promises to you in a clear and decisive way.

_____

_____

_____

_____

_____

_____

_____

_____

_____

_____

_____

_____

_____

_____

*One of the reasons for our sense of futility
in prayer is that we have lost our power to
visualize.... The power of visualization is
what God gives a saint so that he can go
beyond himself and be firmly placed into
relationships he never before experienced.*

Oswald Chambers

You Shall Dream Dreams (Imagination)

And it shall come to pass afterward, that I will pour out my spirit upon all flesh; and your sons and your daughters shall prophesy, your old men shall dream dreams, your young men shall see visions. **Joel 2:28 (KJV)**

Arthur watched his friend's eyes grow wide with excitement as the car turned off the main highway and onto a dusty drive. To the east Arthur saw the shimmering silver snow-capped slopes of the San Bernardino Mountains. To the west, a copper sun sank into the Pacific Ocean. Beyond the hood of the car lay 160 acres of dirt.

His friend pointed through the windshield. "Right over there, Arthur, where those trees begin—that'll be yours."

"It's a big field of dirt clods."

"'Of course it's a field. That's why it's cheap."

"I don't know, Walt. The sellers want a lot of money for

acres and acres of dirt."

"You're not buying dirt. You're buying a dream. There's a fortune to be made here, you'll see."

"Tell me again how this park of yours is going to work."

Walt turned off the engine and stepped out. Arthur followed, wishing now he'd kept his mouth shut.

"It's not going to be just any park. It'll be magical."

"Right. An enchanted amusement park," Arthur said.

"Think of it more as a kingdom. It'll have a castle and moat, guards, wizards, princes, and princesses."

Arthur said, "You got a name for this park?"

"Mouse Park."

"You're kidding, right? Who's going to pay to come play in a mouse park?"

"Okay, we'll work on the name. This'll be a place where dreams come true. I have the plans all right here, in my head."

"Why not put your tiny town in that clearing?" said Arthur, pointing toward a wide swath of tumbleweeds and sagebrush. "That way, you wouldn't have to knock down as many trees."

"My Wild West settlement goes on that plot."

"I suppose it'll have cowboys and horses and gun fighters."

"Wouldn't be much of a frontier village without those, now would it?"

"I wish I had your vision, Walt, I really do."

"You can. You just have to believe."*

Too often we see life through the tiny periscope of our past

* *Superhuman Performance: Utilizing Your Gifts to Perform at Extraordinary Levels* by Darrayl and Derrick Miles, Raleigh, NC: Milestone Publishing House, 2012. Used by permission.

failures. Fear and friends warn us to turn back from the dream God placed within our hearts. The prophet Joel spoke of a time when God would pour out His Spirit on His people and infuse them with new visions. The wonderful thing about serving a living God is that He takes the initiative to inspire us with His power. If the dream is *only* ours, we'll tire and quit. But when God gives us a vision and we respond by saying "yes," we can change the world.

Walt Disney wasn't the sort of man who let a dream die. How about us? Is God calling us to a dream? Let's stretch out our hands and touch the stars.

Discern: Read Joel 2:21-29. What rains has God sent recently to nourish your dream? Are you responding with gratitude and action?

_____

_____

_____

_____

_____

_____

_____

Do: Explain what you would *like* God to do for you in 4-5 sentences. Then pray, "Thy will be done." Return to God with your request often and constantly lean forward in obedience.

_____

_____

_____

_____

_____

_____

_____

_____

_____

_____

_____

_____

God will never reveal more truth about Himself to you, until you have obeyed what you know already. **Oswald Chambers**

A Widow's Might
(Sacrifice)

Jesus sat down opposite the place where the offerings were put and watched the crowd putting their money into the temple treasury. Many rich people threw in large amounts. But a poor widow came and put in two very small copper coins, worth only a fraction of a penny. Calling his disciples to him, Jesus said, "I tell you the truth, this poor widow has put more into the treasury than all the others. They all gave out of their wealth; but she, out of her poverty, put in everything— all she had to live on. **Mark 12:41-44 (NIV)**

God's accounting practices do not work in corporate America or with family budgets. For God, a full day's work is counted the same as part-time piddling. Two copper coins are worth more than a sack of gold. What looks like laziness, Jesus considers devotion: "Mary has chosen the better part," He said in Luke

10:42, "and it will not be taken from her." Those who are given much will receive more, while those who hoard the little they have are cast into darkness.

"When God wants me to give more, He'll give me more money, more time, more resources." That's the cry of those too stressed to feel the warmth of God's embrace.

Perhaps more *is* the solution, but the Scriptures suggest a different accounting method. "We are hard pressed on every side," the apostle Paul wrote in 2 Corinthians 4:8, "but not crushed; perplexed, but not in despair; persecuted, but not abandoned; struck down, but not destroyed." Paul's words are hardly an endorsement for the "give me more and I'll do more" approach to God's work. If we say, "When God wants me to... He will...," we are really claiming that He has not done enough, loved enough, or died enough to satisfy us.

The many "threw in" their wealth. The widow "put in" all she had.

Have we? Have we put our whole heart into the task to which we've been called? Have we put in the time necessary to carry forward His message of hope and life? Or are we waiting for a greater calling, heartier encouragement, or a larger field of work?

God often begins with menial assignments, tiny tithes, and insignificant gestures. In the small matters His kingdom's economy prospers. God has given us *all* we need. We only need to give back *all* we have.

Discern: Read 2 Kings 5:1-14. Why do you think Naaman and his wife followed the advice of the "young girl from Israel"?

_____

_____

_____

_____

_____

_____

_____

_____

_____

_____

Do: What small tasks has God given you? Are you putting your whole heart into completing them?

_____

_____

_____

_____

_____

_____

_____

_____

_____

_____

_____

_____

When I stop telling God what I want, He can catch me up for what he wants.... He simply asks me to have implicit faith in Himself and in His goodness.

Oswald Chambers

From Pit to Prominence
(Faithfulness)

So the warden put Joseph in charge of all those held in the prison, and he was made responsible for all that was done there. **Genesis 39:22 (NIV)**

In his thirties he led an e-business technology team from a start-up company to its public stock offering. The firm made a splash in the press, sold out, and went looking for a new and younger manager.

Unemployed, he founded a new business. The job took him to Asia where he met with top executives in the semi-conductor industry. Modeling the successful strategy of his previous job, he positioned the firm to go public. But days before their announcement, the global economy burped, investors pulled back, and the firm floundered. For years he watched as one angel investor after another waltzed by his office, but none came bearing good news and gifts. The firm folded.

In order to pay the bills, he began restoring homes, adding

decks, and refinishing rooms. Of course, business thrived. He hired additional help, rebuilt his savings, and discovered that he enjoyed working with his hands, going to bed tired, and waking up in better shape than the day before. He dropped pounds and added muscle, plus a few more clients. Over coffee one morning, a customer commented on his leadership skills. "Would you like to have a job with an office, benefits, and stock options?" his friend asked.

"Only if it presents a challenge."

Of course it would.

He accepted a job at the customer's firm and soon his unit led the company in growth, profits, and efficiency. The CEO offered him a promotion, one as head of a new division with increased responsibility and income. Then, on the eve of the announcement, he was diagnosed with bone cancer. The firm fired him.

Joseph also suffered betrayal, mistreatment, and misfortune. Told by God that he would become a grand leader, Joseph struggled with the mantle of greatness. "Listen to the dream I had," said Joseph. "I had another dream.... No one is greater in this house than I am.... When all goes well with you, remember me...show me kindness...mention me...I have done nothing to deserve being put in a pit." Joseph's arrogant attitude bred jealousy and resentment, leading others to forget and forsake him.

God has made each of us responsible for someone and some thing. Whether we're serving time in prison, serving soup to the homeless, or serving on the board of a Fortune 500 company, our attitude toward others reflects our heart for God's work. When my friend arrived home that final evening, he hugged his wife, held her hand, and prayed for God to see them through the crisis—just as they'd done in times past. I have no doubt he'll rise again from pit to prominence. That's what men of God do.

Even when we feel imprisoned, we don't have to yield to despair. God's promises, power, and protection will set us free if we trust, work, and wait upon Him.

Discern: Read Genesis 39:1-23. How did God demonstrate both His power and His protection in Joseph's life? How do we know that Joseph placed his confidence in God's promises?

_____

_____

_____

_____

_____

_____

_____

_____

Do: Place your confidence in God's promises this week by completing a task that no one but you and God will see.

_____

_____

_____

_____

_____

_____

_____

_____

_____

_____

_____

_____

Some extraordinary thing happens to a man who holds on to the love of God when the odds are all against God's character.

Oswald Chambers

Plumb the Depths of God's Love (Gratitude)

If you, then, though you are evil, know how to give good gifts to your children, how much more will your Father in heaven give good gifts to those who ask him! **Matthew 7:11 (NIV)**

Days before his college graduation, a young man visited a car dealership. For years he had longed to own a red sports car. Knowing his father could easily pay cash for the car, the son shared his secret desire with his dad. Days later, with diploma in hand, the boy's father called him into the study. The father told his son how proud he was of him and how much he loved him. Then the man handed the boy a beautifully wrapped present. Eagerly, the young man ripped away the silver paper. Inside he found, not a set of car keys, but a new leather-bound Bible with his name embossed in gold on the cover.

"A Bible? You bought me a book?" The young man slammed the gift down on his father's desk and stormed out of the study.

Years passed. The boy became successful in business and purchased a red sports car with his own money. He married his college sweetheart, built her a beautiful home, and started a family. Not once did he return his dad's phone messages—not even when he learned his father was sick. Finally at his wife's insistence, he reluctantly packed a suitcase and went home.

He parked his red sports car behind an ambulance and rushed into the study, but he was too late. His father lay on the couch, a sheet over his body. Struggling to remain stoic the boy waited until the paramedics departed. Then sinking into his father's chair behind the maple desk he took in the smells: the scent of his father's cologne and the sweet aroma of cigars. On the corner of the desk he spied his graduation present—its silver wrapping paper torn and crumpled, just as he'd left it all those years ago. Removing the Bible, he turned to a bookmarked page and began to read:

If you, then, though you are evil, know how to give good gifts to your children, how much more will your Father in heaven give good gifts to those who ask him!

The verse had been underlined, initialed, and dated by his dad. A sticky note was affixed beneath the Scripture. On it was a VIN number and the name of a salesman at the car dealership. Under the crude drawing of a convertible sports car were the words: "I'm proud of you, son. May you find God's rich blessings in all your endeavors."

We cannot earn God's love by following denominational rules or religious tenets. He does not love us more because of our good works or love us less when we turn our backs on Him.

God loved you before there *was* a you. Loved you while you hated Him. Loves you still.

Too often we settle for work we can do, instead of striving for the work to which we're called. Jesus makes it clear: God gives good gifts to those who ask. Have we asked? Has He placed an impossible desire within our heart? If so, the excitement we feel could be God's Spirit pounding on the door of our heart.

God loves us and gives good gifts to those who ask. That's all we *really* need to know about His work. The rest we'll find in the owner's manual.

Discern: Read Matthew 7:7-11. What good gifts has God given you? What situation in your life do you consider a burden rather than a gift?

_____

_____

_____

_____

_____

_____

_____

Do: Give one of your burdens to the Lord. Ask Him to transform it into a gift.

_____

_____

_____

_____

_____

_____

_____

_____

_____

_____

_____

_____

_____

_____

Do not expect God always to give you His thrilling minutes, but learn to live in the domain of drudgery by the power of God.
Oswald Chambers

Consecrated to Christ
(Service)

So whether you eat or drink or whatever you do,
do it all for the glory of God.
1 Corinthians 10:31 (NIV)

Over two thousand years ago, a father chose the greatest scholar of his age to tutor his young son in liberal arts. The gifted instructor taught the boy architecture, music, literature, politics, and natural sciences. A few years later, the boy, barely in his twenties, set out to conquer the world. He did. By the age of thirty, he had created one of the largest empires known to man, stretching from the Ionian Sea to the Himalayas. He was undefeated in battle and remains one of history's most successful commanders. Alexander the Great died at the age of thirty-two. Many of his contemporaries considered him a drunk and a womanizer.

Three centuries after Alexander's death, another Father sent His Son out to conquer the world. He taught His boy to lead through serving, win through losing Himself for others, and achieve victory through loving His enemies. He, too, died around the age of thirty-two. Today His victory over death remains the greatest conquest known to man.

The Hebrew word *hanakh* means "to dedicate" or "to consecrate." Once Christ dedicated His life to following the will of His Father, He could do nothing other than become victorious.

Whatever our hands find to do, we consecrate to God. We ask, "Lord, is this opportunity from you? Did you place this dream in my heart?" If He affirms this "nudging" through Scripture, the wise counsel of godly friends, and confirming circumstances, then we seek ways to use this new work to help others. If God is in the task, He will bless the work of our hands.

Discern: Read 1 Corinthians 10:23-33. What guidelines does Paul give for effective service?

_____

_____

_____

_____

_____

_____

_____

_____

Do: Take an inventory of your habits. Is there something you need to eliminate so that you can serve God and others more effectively?

_____

_____

_____

_____

_____

_____

_____

_____

_____

_____

_____

_____

_____

_____

Do we appreciate the miraculous salvation of Jesus Christ enough to be our utmost for His highest – our best for His glory? **Oswald Chambers**

Walking in Integrity
(Purity)

Whoever walks in integrity walks securely, but he
who makes his ways crooked will be found out.
Proverbs 10:9 (ESV)

A cigar smoker purchased several hundred expensive stogies and had them insured against fire. After he'd smoked them all, he filed a claim, pointing out that the cigars had gone up in flames. The company refused to pay and the man sued. A judge ruled that because the insurance company had agreed to insure the cigars against fire, it was legally responsible. The company paid the claim. When the man accepted the money, the company had him arrested for arson.

The writer of Proverbs says the crooked will be found out. We live in a transparent society. More than any time in history, our sins are exposed to others. You might think getting caught would be a deterrent. Instead, we have grown numb to our outlandish acts of disobedience and lewdness. Like the man with the cigars, we brazenly seek to bend the rules to our advantage.

But God calls us to a higher standard: one of holiness and honor. Left to our own desires we are indeed wretched. With Christ we are wrecked men and women under repair.

This year, this week, this day we can resolve to walk in integrity. We can ask God to transform us into encouragers, not faultfinders—people who speak good news and hope, not bitterness. We can practice fairness in our business dealings and deliver more than what is required. This is the foundation of both sound business and godly living.

Discern: Read 2 Samuel 15:1-12. What dishonest tactics did Absalom use to usurp his father's throne? What was the outcome? (2 Samuel 18:14-15)

_____

_____

_____

_____

_____

_____

_____

Do: Examine your interaction with family members and/or co-workers. How can you improve your integrity?

_____

_____

_____

_____

_____

_____

_____

_____

_____

_____

_____

_____

_____

_____

If you have ever had a vision from God,
you may try as you will to be satisfied on
a lower level, but God will never allow it.
Oswald Chambers

The Future Isn't What It Used to Be (Vision)

For nothing is impossible with God.
Luke 1:37 (NIV)

In 1890 Bishop Wright preached on the impending return of Christ. He said everything God had sent man to do on earth was done. A member of the congregation jumped to his feet and predicted that some day man would fly. The bishop responded with the infamous line: "If God had intended man to fly, he would have given him wings."

When we view the whole of creation, we realize God's work was indeed good—and incomplete. He did not give us wings with which to fly, replacement parts for failing organs, or antibodies for deadly diseases. His creative work is a beginning; our job is to continue His work by subduing, improving, and imagining what can be from what is not—yet. When Mary asked, "How will this be?" the angel of God replied, "Nothing is impossible with God."

When we follow God wholeheartedly, we no longer bemoan what was or what isn't—we anticipate what will be. "The call of God is like the call of the sea," wrote Oswald Chambers. "No one hears it except the person who has the nature of the sea in him." This call begins with the transforming work of Christ's Spirit within us. When we allow Him to lead, possibilities abound.

Thirteen years after Bishop Wright preached on the impending return of Christ, his two sons, Orville and Wilbur, made the first powered flight by man at Kitty Hawk. What impossible task lies ahead of us? Sometimes all we need is another bump or jump and the quiet confidence that God has called us to the task.

Discern: Read Ezekiel 37:1-14. What point was God making by showing His prophet the valley of dry bones? What did He command Ezekiel to do?

_____

_____

_____

_____

_____

_____

_____

Do: What dry bones lie before you? What is God commanding you to do? Be mindful of Scripture verses that continue to come up in conversations, in sermons, and in your quiet time.

_____

_____

_____

_____

_____

_____

_____

_____

_____

_____

_____

If my relationship to Him is that of love, I will do what He says without any hesitation. If I hesitate, it is because I love someone else in competition with Him, viz., myself. **Oswald Chambers**

My Wig Is Not That Big
(Influence)

Jabez cried out to the God of Israel, "Oh, that you would bless me and enlarge my territory! Let your hand be with me, and keep me from harm so that I will be free from pain." And God granted his request. **1 Chronicles 4:10 (NIV)**

Agnes Bojaxhiu's father died when she was eight years old. Agnes never went to college, never married, and never owned a car. At eighteen, she left home and never saw her mother or sister again. When she was thirty-six, she received a "call within the call": "I was to leave and help the poor while living among them. It was an order. To fail would have been to break the faith."* Agnes wasn't a big wig, but through her faith in a big God Agnes, known worldwide as Mother Teresa, extended her work far beyond the borders of her humble beginnings.

His mother died when he was nine years old. In 1832 he ran for state legislature and finished eighth in a field of thirteen candidates. The following year he and a partner opened a general store, but the business failed. He sought to become speaker of the state legislature and lost. He applied for the job of land officer but was denied. In 1858 he missed a seat in the U.S. Senate when his party failed to win control of the state legislature. Then in 1860 he became the 16th president of the United States and God's shepherd for a divided nation. Of the war that cost him his life, he said, "I am almost ready to say that this is probably true, that God wills this contest."** Abraham Lincoln wasn't a big wig either, but through his obedience he united a nation and extended the borders of freedom to an enslaved people.

What borders are we bumping against? How is God challenging us to expand our area of influence? When we ask God to expand our borders for Him, we may find that it consumes us. Great endeavors often will. Nevertheless, when we serve others selflessly, we are most like Christ.

We may not be big wigs, but the size of our wig matters less than the size of our heart. First, we ask for God's blessing. Then we seek ways to expand our area of influence for Him.

---

*<http://www.motherteresacause.info/ABriefBiography.htm>
**<http://americanhistory.about.com/od/abrahamlincoln/p/plincoln.htm>

Discern: Read Joshua 14:6-12. Caleb wanted to extend his borders. What gave him the confidence he needed?

_____

_____

_____

_____

_____

_____

_____

Do: When God provides an opportunity to act on the knowledge and inclination He has placed within your heart, step out in faith. Do not delay. This could be His way of testing you to see if you can handle all that He wants to give you.

_____

_____

_____

_____

_____

_____

_____

_____

_____

_____

_____

_____

The voice of the Spirit of God is as gentle
as a summer breeze—so gentle that unless
you are living in complete fellowship and
oneness with God, you will never hear it.

Oswald Chambers

Marching Orders
(Discernment)

*For this reason, since the day we heard about you,
we have not stopped praying for you and asking
God to fill you with the knowledge of his will
through all spiritual wisdom and understanding.*
Colossians 1:9 (NIV)

On December 26, 1944, Japanese Intelligence Officer Hiroo Onoda, arrived on Lubang Island in the Philippines. Onoda's orders were to disrupt the enemy's attempts to secure the island. But before he could destroy the airstrip and blow up the pier, American forces captured Lubang Island. Onoda and three other Japanese soldiers fled to the hills and hid.

They were still hiding a year later when Onoda recovered a leaflet that read, "The war ended on August 15. Come down from the mountains!" Onoda refused. His orders were clear. Under no circumstances was he to surrender.

Unable to reach his superiors, Onoda and his men burrowed

deeper into the hills. In 1949, one of the men surrendered to Filipino forces. A few years later an aircraft dropped letters and pictures from Onoda's family, urging him to come down. Still he refused. In 1954 members of a search party accidentally killed one of his men. Twenty years later local police mistakenly shot the last of his comrades. Now only Onoda remained, alone and forgotten, fighting a war he'd already lost.

How often have we acted like Hiroo Ono—refusing to leave an obsolete job or way of life after God's Spirit has relocated? In fear we clutch complacency in our fists, mistrusting the Spirit's call and God's whispering voice: "Let go. I've moved. Join me over here." Desperately grasping for what's already lost, we burrow into caves of depression. The darkness of despair and isolation engulfs us. Sensing that we've missed out on life's best, regret claws at our heart.

If we are to win our daily battles, we must do more than wear the armor of God. We must daily receive our marching orders from God and be ready to move out when He calls us to a new mission. In the same way, we must also be prepared to give up the work we thought was ours alone. There is no "our." There is only "His." God doesn't change, but His plans for us do change.

On March 9, 1974, Onoda emerged from the jungle. He surrendered his uniform, sword, rifle, hand grenades, and 500 rounds of ammunition. He'd already surrendered thirty years of his life to isolation and fear.

Don't be like Onoda. Pray daily. Check in each morning with your Commander. Be prepared to break camp and march forward.

Discern: Read Isaiah 6:1-13. What motivated Isaiah to say, "Here am I, send me"? What did God ask him to do?

_____

_____

_____

_____

_____

_____

_____

_____

_____

Do: Before you get out of bed each morning, ask your Commander in Chief, "What are your orders for me today?"

_____

_____

_____

_____

_____

_____

_____

_____

_____

_____

_____

_____

_____

There is a "darkness" that comes from
too much light—that is a time to listen.
Oswald Chambers

A Self-Made Man
(Endurance)

I have been deprived of peace; I have forgotten
what prosperity is. **Lamentations 3:17 (NIV)**

He left his job with $40,000 in the bank and freelance projects worth $5000. A year later he was broke. The bank placed his condo up for auction. He began packing boxes although he had no money to pay for storage. He tried finding part-time work, but when potential employers saw his resumé, they labeled him "too gifted" and "overqualified" for such menial work.

"I have been deprived of peace; I have forgotten what prosperity is." Money may not buy happiness, but it *can* buy an improved level of misery.

Working in God's kingdom may involve lean times. Do no despair. Hardship can serve as a necessary tool, shaping us into the employees God desires. But our own rebellion and pride can also lead to times of hunger.

The prophet Jeremiah, who wrote Lamentations, considered

the ways of God's people and saw His hand in their punishment. They had willfully disobeyed, refusing to recognize their missteps and to repent. They knew a "better" way, and their way proved bitter.

_____Declaring God's plan for our future without first consulting Him is foolish. Considering the cost of His calling and staying close to Him is wise. We cannot think of ourselves as "self-made" men and women. The root of all evil is believing that security, peace, and salvation comes through *our* efforts, through *our* love of money and safety.

I don't know what happened to the man who left his job at the bank. Perhaps he found temporary sanctuary in a previous career. He may have paid his bills and remained in his condo. Maybe his financial storm has passed. But I do know this: God gifted him in ways others can only dream of. This man's artistic talents could fill a museum if only he had the time and money to pursue his dream.

Regardless of our current economic condition, if we remain obedient to God's call, we can rest in the peace of knowing we've done our best.

Discern: Read Lamentations 3:1-33. What truths about God sustained Jeremiah during his lean times?

_____

_____

_____

_____

_____

_____

_____

_____

Do: What truths about God bolster your confidence in lean times? Write them down. Post them in a place where you will see them every day.

_____

_____

_____

_____

_____

_____

_____

_____

_____

_____

_____

_____

Growth in grace stops the moment I get huffed. **Oswald Chambers**

Roast Yourself
(Humility)

Who out there fears God, actually listens to the voice of his servant? For anyone out there who doesn't know where you're going, anyone groping in the dark, Here's what: Trust in God. Lean on your God! But if all you're after is making trouble, playing with fire, Go ahead and see where it gets you. Set your fires, stir people up, blow on the flames, But don't expect me to just stand there and watch. I'll hold your feet to those flames. **Isaiah 50:11 (MSG)**

In the mid-eighties, following Band Aid's recording project, "Do They Know It's Christmas?", Harry Belafonte teamed up with fundraiser Ken Kragen to assemble some of the top names in the recording industry. Their goal was to create a hit record and then donate the proceeds to the African famine relief project. Within days pop stars like Stevie Wonder, Paul Simon,

Billy Joel, Willie Nelson, Bruce Springsteen, Kenny Loggins, and Bob Dylan arrived at Kenny Rogers' Lion Share Recording Studio. A few months later the super-group released "We Are the World." The song became the fastest-selling American pop single in history. Sales exceeded twenty million copies. Along with promotional and merchandise products, the project raised over $63 million in humanitarian aid.*

But the song might never have been created if the performers hadn't shelved their egos and agreed to work as a team to benefit others. Secrecy and tight security kept the group focused on the larger good, not their own agendas.

The public loves a good fight. Tabloids tout celebrity spats, political rancor, and company feuds. We feast on negative news. But God says a man who stirs up trouble will roast himself on the hot coals he stokes for others—that he's playing with fire when he stirs up trouble.

A few days before the musicians gathered in the studio, Lionel Richie posted a sign over the entrance that read: "Check your ego at the door."

Those who lead best, check their ego at the door.

---

*http://en.wikipedia.org/wiki/We_Are_the_World

Discern: Read Luke 14:7-11. What is the point of Jesus' parable?

_____

_____

_____

_____

_____

_____

_____

Do: Check your ego at the door the next time you enter your church or workplace and perform a menial task like picking up trash or wiping down a bathroom countertop. Make it habit.

_____

_____

_____

_____

_____

_____

_____

_____

_____

_____

_____

_____

_____

Our Lord has a right to expect that those who name His name have an underlying confidence in Him. **Oswald Chambers**

Worst Case Scenarios
(Tenacity)

When life is heavy and hard to take, go off by yourself. Enter the silence. Bow in prayer. Don't ask questions: Wait for hope to appear. Don't run from trouble. Take it full-face. The "worst" is never the worst. **Lamentations 3:28-30 (MSG)**

"What's the worst that could happen?" he asked the college admissions officer.

"You could flunk out."

"Not if you won't let me in, I can't. Please, sir, isn't there some place you can put me?"

The young man sat in the admissions office, hoping for a chance to attend college. That's all he needed, just a shot. But a look of disgust spread across the face of the person reviewing his transcripts.

"Son, I'd like to help, but honestly, you have no business at this university. Worse, you have no hope of graduating."

The young man persisted and was finally offered admittance in the university's Industrial Arts Program. "Industrial Arts it is," he replied, grateful for any chance at college—even one in art.

The Old Testament writer laments: "Life is heavy." Amen to that. But the writer also offers advice for how we are to deal with life's adversities.

- Seek solitude
- Pray
- Trust God's goodness
- Face adversity with a full-on, in-your-face tenacity
- Don't ask "why me?"
- Risk a trip into the unknown
- Forget about the how, when, and where. Simply obey His voice, His words, and His Spirit.

Mark Twain once quipped, "I am an old man and have known a great many troubles, but most of them never happened."

What worst-case scenario looms before you? Don't run from it. Seek God in silence, voice your concerns, and wait for His strength. Chances are, the worst-case scenario won't happen. But if it does, you can be certain that God allowed it. And if God allowed it, it will bring about exactly what He wants to accomplish in accordance with His divine will.

Discern: Read Philippians 1:1-11. What is God's goal for our lives? What has He guaranteed?

_____

_____

_____

_____

_____

_____

_____

_____

_____

Do: Every time you're tempted to moan about a worst-case scenario, say "God knows what He's doing" instead.

_____

_____

_____

_____

_____

_____

_____

_____

_____

_____

_____

_____

_____

We have to be exceptional in the ordinary things, to be holy in mean streets, among mean people, and this is not learned in five minutes. **Oswald Chambers**

Prepare to Wait
(Diligence)

Make the most of every opportunity.
Colossians 4:5a (MSG)

Even though he led his high school team to a state championship, no college offered him an athletic scholarship. Harvard said that he *might* be able to play for them—but he would have to pay his way.

During his sophomore season he averaged 12.6 points and was named All-Ivy League Second Team. By his junior year, he was the only NCAA Division I men's basketball player who ranked in the top ten in his conference for scoring, rebounding, assists, steals, blocked shots, field goal percentage, free throw percentage, and three-point shot percentage. ESPN called him "one of the twelve most versatile players in college basketball."* But professional scouts were not impressed. On the day of the NBA draft, no one called his name. The Golden State Warriors finally offered him a partial contract but released him a few months later. He bounced around to a couple of other teams before falling into the development league.

Then he received "the call." The New York Knicks needed him to play starting guard while their star player recovered from his injuries. In his first four NBA starts he scored more points than any player in NBA history, surpassing Allen Iverson, Shaquille O'Neal, and Michael Jordan. With him on the floor, the struggling Knicks became unstoppable. He produced game winning shots and triggered a seven game winning streak. Jeremy Lin continues to shoot over thirty percent from three-point range and average around 15 points per game. He is professional sports' "Linsation."

The Apostle Paul directs us to make the most of every opportunity, not make do or make excuses. When tossed into prison, Joseph the Dreamer changed the culture of captivity. When sent into the fields, Ruth gleaned more than grain—she gathered a husband. Peter, when told to fish for men, founded a church. What door of opportunity has God placed before you?

Pastor David Jeremiah writes in his best selling book, *Life Wide Open*, "God's open doors are often disguised as problems, time-sensitive, met with resistance, and often missed because of fear."** Are you afraid, stuck, and overwhelmed by difficulties? If so, practice, prepare, and pray for an opportunity to shine for Him.

Good things come to those who wait—great things come to those who prepare *while* they wait.

---

* http://www.gocrimson.com/sports/mbkb/2009-10/releases/ 091007_Lin_ESPN
**Jeremiah, David. *Life Wide Open*. Nashville: Thomas Nelson, 2005.

Discern: Read Daniel 1. What did Daniel and his friends do in preparation for their new jobs as servants in Babylon?

_____

_____

_____

_____

_____

_____

_____

_____

Do: What spiritual exercises do you do every day to prepare for the battles you will surely face as a servant of God?

_____

_____

_____

_____

_____

_____

_____

_____

_____

_____

_____

_____

_____

God does not give us overcoming life—
He gives us life as we overcome.

Oswald Chambers

Wounded for His Work
(Suffering)

Those who hope in the LORD will renew their strength. They will soar on wings like eagles; they will run and not grow weary, they will walk and not be faint. **Isaiah 40:31 (NIV)**

She stood in the lobby of the cafeteria, tray in hand, feet moving with the slow shuffle of a geriatric patient. Only she wasn't ancient and this wasn't an assisted living home. This building was crowded with authors, agents, and editors hurrying to make appointments, meet deadlines, and catch dreams. When others asked, she spoke candidly about the stroke and how it had changed her life: how she'd been transformed from a vibrant woman into a frail shell.

"I asked why. Over and over I asked why. But when God didn't answer, I changed the question to 'what do you want me to do now, God?'"

What indeed. What do we make of those God wounds? Why did God give Moses a stuttering mouth, Paul a thorn, Jacob a limp, and this woman a journey hampered by small but faithful steps? Isaiah wrote, "Those who hope in the LORD will renew their strength."

"I still struggle but I know He's there for me," she said. "When I hit a 'wall' I give the problem to God. I've learned to trust Him in all things, knowing He'll take care of it in His time. This stroke and my hope in Him allows me to take short steps *with* Him, not past Him."

God promises that those who hope in Him will soar. Every day we need to pray, "Lord, help me to walk and not grow faint, run and not grow weary. Help me soar above my pain."

Today if you find yourself moving too fast, please slow down and thank God that you *can* move too fast.

Discern: Read Isaiah 40:6-31. What enables us to soar even if we have a broken wing?

_____

_____

_____

_____

_____

_____

Do: What short step can you take today that will bring you closer to fulfilling the dream that God has placed within your heart?

_____

_____

_____

_____

_____

_____

_____

_____

_____

_____

_____

_____

All of God's revealed truths are sealed until they are opened to us through obedience. **Oswald Chambers**

Plan Man
(Obedience)

*"For I know the plans I have for you," declares
the LORD, "plans to prosper you and not to harm
you, plans to give you hope and a future. Then you
will call upon me and come and pray to me, and
I will listen to you."* **Jeremiah 29:11-12 (NIV)**

My son, I planned you before the creation of the world; I
created you to walk with me in the cool of the day. But you loved
a lie more than Truth, so I shaped a new plan, one that would
redeem you from your wandering. I came to you in dreams and
visions and whispered my plan to you, but you refused to listen
and were carried into bondage. Because you worshiped gods of
gold, wood, and stubble, you lived as an alien in a foreign land.

When you acknowledged the futility of your plan and called
to me, I came. I showed you my glory and delivered you from
slavery. I gave you my law and prophets, fed you, clothed you,
and led you into a land of promise. But you preferred the lies of

spies. I gave you cities you did not build and lands you did not plow—still you refused my rest.

I allowed you to be taken captive and when you cried out to me, I listened, drawing you to me. Still you would not be held; you refused to be consoled. You returned to my land a stiff-necked rebel. And when you were secure in your walled cities and fat on the grain you did not plant, once more you cast aside my plan.

So I sent my Son, my only Son. *Perhaps they will listen to Him*, I thought. But you preferred violence to peace, your pride to my love. You killed my Boy—but not my plan.

And now, oh man, your end is near. Frail and broken, your eyes dim. With dry lips you gasp for breath. Listen, oh man, if you can. Receive my words. I have a plan, a plan to nourish you and not harm you—a plan to give you hope and a future. My plan is good because I am good. Come near to me, oh man, and I will whisper once more. Pray to me and hear my words.

I love you, man. That's my plan. That's all you need to know.

Discern: Read Jeremiah 29:1-14. Jeremiah is writing to Jewish exiles in Babylon. What does he tell them to do? Why are they to do it?

_____

_____

_____

_____

_____

_____

Do: What contribution can you make to the "peace and prosperity" of the place to which God has carried you—even if you're there against your will?

_____

_____

_____

_____

_____

_____

_____

_____

_____

_____

_____

_____

_____

God gives us a vision, and then He takes us down to the valley to batter us into the shape of that vision. It is in the valley that so many of us give up and faint. Every God-given vision will become real if we will only have patience.

Oswald Chambers

God As Your Talent Agent
(Patience)

Since before time began no one has ever imagined, no ear heard, no eye seen, a God like you who works for those who wait for him. You meet those who happily do what is right, who keep a good memory of the way you work. **Isaiah 64:4 (MSG)**

The best-selling book, *The Day of the Jackal*, was turned down with the comment of "no reader interest." The book has since sold eight million copies. *The Diary of Anne Frank* was rejected 15 times and called "very dull," filled with unfamiliar characters who bickered like a typical family. *Chicken Soup for the Soul* by Jack Canfield and Mark Victor Hansen was rejected 140 times. And *Carrie* by Stephen King? Rejected 30 times. Supposedly, after the final rejection, King threw the manuscript in the trash and his wife fished it out.

What does it mean to wait for God? Does it mean "wait on," as in serve Him? Or "wait for," the way we might wait at a customer service desk?

Man lives for the moment; God lives for the ages. We want success right now; God wants us right with Him. We hope God will give us our dreams; He dreams of a time when we no longer look to Him as the giver of gifts and blessings but simply as Lord.

When faced with the urgency of "now," consider what it means to "wait upon God." We are not called to sit and do nothing. We are called to wait. Wait—as in serve Him. Wait—as in serve others. Wait as only a servant can wait when he works with all his heart to do the work his Master has called him to do.

We wait upon the Lord with the skills we have and the passion He's placed in our heart. In doing so, we discover that His eyes and ears are roaming the earth looking for other ways that He can promote us into greater service for Him.

Discern: Joshua served Moses for forty years before he was equipped to take Moses' place. Why did God choose Joshua? Study Exodus 17:8-16, 33:7-11 and Numbers 14:1-10.

_____

_____

_____

_____

_____

_____

Do: Seek the counsel of others who you consider leaders—people who are frank, perceptive, and deeply committed to prayer. They may have a word from God that you may not have heard.

_____

_____

_____

_____

_____

_____

_____

_____

_____

_____

_____

_____

Once you face the strain, you will immediately get the strength.

Oswald Chambers

What's Your Excuse?
(Power)

I can do everything through him who gives me strength. **Philippians 4:13 (NIV)**

At the age of 40, Harland David Sanders began serving fried chicken from his service station. Within a few years his diner moved into a nearby motel, but the restaurant failed when a new Interstate siphoned away customers. Rather than retreat and retire, Sanders took $105 from his first Social Security check and began looking for ways to expand his business. When he died in 1980, "Colonel" Sanders had turned Kentucky Fried Chicken into a household name. What's your excuse for giving up?

The Wright brothers were aware that no one had ever flown, but they tried anyway. Florence Chadwick knew the names of those who died trying to swim the English Channel, but she plunged in and reached the shores of France. David was too young, untested, and poorly equipped to face Goliath, but he ran into the fight. What are you waiting for?

"Nobody gets to run the mill by doing run-of-the-mill work," wrote Thomas J. Frye,* and yet God does his best work through mill workers. It is the common man and woman who toil away in menial jobs, projecting the Good News—sometimes through words, but often through acts of service, joy, and empathy. The adage is true: "God doesn't call the equipped; He equips the called."

Paul told the church in Philippi that he could do all things through Christ. Not *for* Christ or *with* Christ but *through* Christ. The power resides within the Spirit. If we are to tap into His supernatural source and accomplish the vision He's placed within us, we must lead by leaning forward, taking risks, and advancing into hostile areas. We *can* do all things through Him who gives us strength, but God cannot force us to act against our will.

When the work seems too hard, we fall to our knees. When the load grows heavy, we lift our arms in praise. When the problems exceed our understanding, we give thanks because He's the solution. Our work in His kingdom has eternal value so God says, "Get to work."

---

* <http://www.random-quotes.com/43/4/43450.html>

Discern: Read 2 Corinthians 4:8-18. What hardships did Paul experience? What prevented him from "losing heart"?

_____

_____

_____

_____

_____

_____

_____

Do: What have you been procrastinating? Make a list. Then ask God for the strength to do those things one by one.

_____

_____

_____

_____

_____

_____

_____

_____

_____

_____

_____

_____

_____

Every relationship that is not based on faithfulness to Himself will end in disaster.
Oswald Chambers

Lean on Him: The Author's Testimonial (Experience)

The book of the genealogy of Jesus Christ, the Son of David, the Son of Abraham: Abraham begot Isaac, Isaac begot Jacob, and Jacob begot Judah and his brothers. **Matthew 1:1-2 (NKJV)**

A few months back I stood shoulder-to-shoulder with best-selling author Bruce Wilkinson. Bruce stood behind a partition, waiting to go on stage. I stood beside Bruce, straining to hear God's voice. Neither of us spoke to the other but we both shared a common bond: we'd failed our way to success.

Bruce explained to the audience how his first magazine folded after just five issues. "When that first magazine ceased publication, I was certain of only one thing," Bruce said. "I'd never produce another magazine." Some months later he did produce another periodical, albeit reluctantly. In 1978 Bruce Wilkinson launched *Daily Walk* and his ministry as a writer, speaker, and publisher took flight. "Had that first magazine succeeded, I might have been tempted to take credit for its success and that of *Daily Walk*. But that failure left no doubt in my mind as to whom deserved the glory," he said.

I also launched and lost money in publishing ventures. Each experience revealed the limits of my abilities and my need for God's assistance in the planning process.

What does it mean to create and then fail in the thing God has called you to do? What does it mean to beget and *not* have success? Abraham begot Isaac in his old age, but the pause between God's promise and the fulfillment of His purpose *through* Abraham spanned decades, causing the patriarch to doubt the *accuracy* of God's vision, the *faithfulness* of His word, and the *goodness* of God's plan. Through failure I've learned that God's plan in God's time with God's people always produces fruit.

The day after I heard Bruce speak, I walked to the summit of Chimney Rock and stood on the mesa overlooking the terracotta stratus of New Mexico's brown and tan mountains. A cold westerly wind pushed against me, driving me away from the edge of the sheer cliff. This is what we fear: falling, failure, and defeat in all its finality. We near the summit of a calling, a dream, or a vision, and we recoil, afraid we'll slip.

"The problem with the Church," said Bruce, "is too many Christians are afraid of failure. But God rarely makes our fear disappear. Instead, He asks us to be strong and take courage."

Let's be courageous and creative. Let's plant the promises of God in our hearts.

Hold God's hand and start something new for Him. You can't see the edge if you don't lean over. So lean on Him.

Discern: Read Genesis 12:1-8. What new thing did God ask Abraham to do? How did Abraham respond?

_____

_____

_____

_____

_____

_____

_____

Do: What new thing has God been nudging you to do? If you have prayed for a long time that God would move you into the center of His will, believe that is exactly what He is doing. Step forward. Look over the edge.

_____

_____

_____

_____

_____

_____

_____

_____

_____

_____

_____

_____

_____

_____

As long as you have the idea that God will always bless you in answer to prayer, He will do it, but He will never give you the grace of His silence. **Oswald Chambers**

Send Scraps
(Persistence)

A Canaanite woman from that vicinity came to him, crying out, "Lord, Son of David, have mercy on me! My daughter is suffering terribly from demon-possession." Jesus did not answer a word. So his disciples came to him and urged him, "Send her away, for she keeps crying out after us." He answered, "I was sent only to the lost sheep of Israel." The woman came and knelt before him. "Lord, help me!" she said. He replied, "It is not right to take the children's bread and toss it to their dogs." "Yes, Lord," she said, "but even the dogs eat the crumbs that fall from their masters' table." Then Jesus answered, "Woman, you have great faith! Your request is granted." And her daughter was healed from that very hour. **Matthew 15:22-28 (NIV)**

What do you do when God ignores you? Isn't that the fear we live with—the nagging doubt that God really *doesn't* notice, hear, or love us? Worse: What if He's not God at all, but some superstitious myth passed down through the ages by anxious people seeking to create meaning in their desperate lives? Silence.

The bills come due, the test results come back—none of the news is good. So we follow the ritual set before us by pious individuals who promise that if we'll simply pray, believe God's promises, and trust Him, all our cares will melt away. But the problems mount, the world turns cold, and we begin to fear there is more to this business of God than is reported from the pulpits.

Ignored. What do you do when God becomes nothing more than an industry and a slick sales pitch? The Canaanite mother came to Jesus; he answered not a word. You might expect that this man who had fed thousands, healed the sick, and debated with rabbis would have at least told her to go home, to stop wasting His time and hers. Instead, the Teacher ignored her. Though the passage doesn't say so explicitly, we can guess what she might have done next—what we often do when God doesn't respond. She turned to the Church. Others have pursued that route and God's people have responded with "our mission budget is spent...tithes are down...we only give to sanctioned charities...." Silence.

Rejected. What do you do when the Church rejects you? Back she came, desperate this time. *Lord, help me!* "Shall I grovel? Would that help? 'Cause if you want me to, I will. Nothing left to lose but my pride and that's not worth keeping." Silence.

Rebuked. What do you do when Christ calls you a dog and says you're unworthy? "Yes, Lord, but... You are God, You are good, and though I am unworthy, even a dog finds scraps under the Master's table." Silence.

Rewarded. What do you do when Christ pushes back, pins you down, and challenges your faith? He asks you to do only one thing: live as if you believe He is God.

Random testing is a part of the job. Get used to it. Work as if the boss is watching your every move. He is. Work as if you have to prove yourself to Him. You do not. He knows you are unworthy. But sometimes we need to remember to keep asking, keep pleading. Depend less on others and more on God. Above all else pray: *Lord, I hunger for your love, healing, and help. Send scraps.*

Discern: Read Luke 18:1-8. How is this parable similar to the story of the Canaanite woman in Matthew 15? What is the point of both illustrations?

_____

_____

_____

_____

_____

_____

_____

Do: What "scraps" has God provided for you? What can you do with them?

_____

_____

_____

_____

_____

_____

_____

_____

_____

_____

_____

_____

_____

_____

God's mark of approval, whenever you obey Him, is peace. **Oswald Chambers**

Grateful or Full of Regret? (Contentment)

Be thankful in all circumstances, for this is God's
will for you who belong to Christ Jesus.
1 Thessalonians 5:18 (NLT)

In this new economy with its high unemployment, constricted credit, and shuttered homes, finding a silver lining is difficult, but I have glimpsed its ragged edge beneath the clouds of this financial storm. Today's joys lie in simple things, like the solitude of the sun rising over the pines and the rhythmic breathing of an infant nuzzled against its mother's chest. Here, at the edge of tomorrow, the gray day bleeds red with the promise of warmth, light, and hope. Economies may crash and our faith may falter, but the planet continues to spin, unfurling a new day every twenty-four hours.

How will we spend it?

As the economy contracts, we huddle in the fetal position clutching what's left of our savings—scared of the future, forgetting the past. We are not the first to face gray days, only the first of this century. These are the labor pains of new life. We will survive, but we will never be the same. The birthing process leaves stretch marks and scars.

So how *should* we react to the current financial storm? We can cling to ten things that will not change:

1) Gulls do not store up for themselves fish and shrimp, and yet they do not starve. If a bird can find enough food each day, so can a man, a woman, and a child.

2) We cannot alter the earth's rotation or adjust the constellations in the sky, and yet we live comfortably in our skin. Should the planet warm and seas rise, we will adapt to our climate and move to higher ground. We always have.

3) Love is free. Taxed, but still free. Families and friends remain the true source of significance. A life loved and spent on others will outlast any economic downturn.

4) Dreams do not die: they enter a dormant phase. A nut buried becomes an oak. *You* may not see your dreams come true, but that doesn't mean they won't. History abounds with remarkable discoveries birthed from the grave.

5) We matter less than we think we do; we will be missed more than we can imagine. Actions and attitudes matter. Live wisely.

6) Trust begins with an open hand. We cannot reach for the future with a fist. Be wise, be discerning—but trust.

7) We cannot help the sun rise, a sparrow sing, or a rain cloud bloom. We control less than we think we do. Relax, let go, and help those you can.

8) Memories cannot be repossessed or auctioned, so make time for others. That is the currency of life.

9) Spend less but savor more. A meager meal eaten slowly can fill a hungry belly. Give thanks for the small things and do not begrudge the tough times. We can endure more than we think we can. We are made in God's image.

10) Look up. A bowed head will miss the sunrise, the sunset, and the silver lining. Of all God's creatures man stands nearest to heaven, so He calls us to turn our eyes toward the heavens and examine the stars. Each of us is already a star in His eyes.

Give thanks in all circumstances. Gratitude pleases God.

Discern: Read Psalm 145. Write down all the blessings David lists in this psalm.

_____

_____

_____

_____

_____

_____

_____

_____

_____

Do: Write a handwritten thank-you note to someone who has been a "silver lining" during a storm in your life.

_____

_____

_____

_____

_____

_____

_____

_____

_____

_____

_____

To believe is to commit.

Oswald Chambers

A Slam Dunk
(Confidence)

Then Asa called to the LORD his God and said, "LORD, there is no one like you to help the powerless against the mighty. Help us, O LORD our God, for we rely on you, and in your name we have come against this vast army. O LORD, you are our God; do not let man prevail against you." **2 Chronicles 14:11 (NIV)**

March 11, 1983, Atlanta's Omni Arena: "After Lo hits these two free throws I want us to guard the inbound pass, but don't foul." The starting five for N.C. State's basketball team broke from the huddle and walked toward the free-throw lane. At the last second, Coach Jim Valvano is rumored to have pulled point guard Sidney Lowe aside and whispered, "If Lo misses these two shots I want you to..."

An unwavering belief in our abilities may be the key to our

success. That Friday night in Atlanta, freshman Lorenzo Charles and N.C. State needed a confidence boost. State's chance to secure an NCAA bid rested in the hands of a freshman, a player whose free-throw average stood at 67.6%. Odds were that Charles would miss at least one of the shots. Maybe both. He'd never gone to the line with the outcome of a game resting in his hands. Valvano knew Lorenzo Charles needed a shot of confidence, so the coach told the players how to react *after* Charles made his free throws.

King Asa needed a boost of confidence too. Though he'd served God and prospered during a reign of peace, the king's men—armed only with large shields, bows, and spears—faced "a vast army and three hundred chariots." Asa knew the risk of fighting alone. He needed help. "We rely on you," he cried out to God. "You help the powerless. There is none like You. You are our God."

We're prone to think that we can win on our own strength, but our legs grow weary and our nerves fray. We squander our chances for victory, advancement, and promotion by accepting God's accolades as our own. All work is a team sport. Family, friends, and co-workers cheer us on in our profession. They remind us that we are more than the sum of our past; they believe that we can do better and that today, we will.

Charles' first attempt missed the rim—wasn't even close. But his second shot fell through the net and State advanced to the next game. The following week State was crowned ACC Champions, received an NCAA bid, and eventually won the national championship all because of Lorenzo Charles' last-second dunk.

What recent defeat prevents us from believing in God's goodness? What disease, financial setback, or broken relationship threatens to crush our confidence and causes us to cower in fear? God has placed us in His starting line up for a reason. He expects great things of us. When no one else believes we can, God does.

Today let us advance with confidence: we play for an awesome God.

Discern: Read 2 Chronicles 14:9-15. What was the source of Asa's confidence? How did God respond to Asa's prayer?

_____

_____

_____

_____

_____

_____

_____

Do: Move forward confidently in the direction of your dream. If you are truly leaning on God as the source of your strength, He will guide you. If you make a wrong turn, He's big enough to correct any mistake you make.

_____

_____

_____

_____

_____

_____

_____

_____

_____

_____

_____

*Every hope or dream of the human mind
will be fulfilled if it is noble and of God.*
Oswald Chambers

God: The One Percent Solution (Success)

The LORD turned to him and said, "Go in the strength you have and save Israel out of Midian's hand. Am I not sending you?" **Judges 6:14 (NIV)**

When God closes a door, He opens a window. You can jump or be pushed, but out you will go. As one nation under God we appear to be a people teetering on the ledge. Will we fly or fall?

A survey of the cultural landscape might lead some to believe that Christians are not flying; they are fleeing to the hills, caves, and fortresses. Christian book publishers continue to slash payrolls, cancel contracts, and shun new voices. Churches flounder and fold due to soaring debt, dwindling tithes, and an anemic spirit within the Body of Christ. Christian couples split and sue for joint custody, trampling the "peace that passes understanding" on the courthouse steps. Jobless and joyless, we sit in the pews, mouthing the words of "How Great Thou Art" and wondering, as Gideon did: *Why has all this happened to us? Where are all God's wonders that our parents told us about?*

Born into the weakest branch of his family tree, Gideon considered himself to be the runt of the litter, and yet God called him a mighty warrior. Could it be that God views us as mighty warriors, too?

For seven years the raiders of the East pillaged the land, stole crops, killed cattle, and forced Gideon's countrymen to hide in mountain clefts, caves, and forts. Cringing in fear, they slinked away from the battlefield.

Christian businessman Peter J. Daniels notes, "The poverty mentality that has afflicted Christians in wealthy nations is a masterstroke of satanic genius. It has impoverished us for decades. It has denied that every Christian is of royal blood."* Could it be that God is calling us to emerge from our hiding place?

When the angel of the LORD appeared to Gideon, he didn't break out into a praise-and-worship song. He didn't fall face down in wonder. He dared to ask, "If I have found favor in your eyes, give me a sign that it is really you talking to me." Are we waiting for a sign from God that He is calling us?

Any encounter with a living God will change us. Gideon received a new title: "Mighty Warrior." He received a new mission: "Strike down the enemy." He received God's power: "I will be with you." He received God's blessing: "Go in the strength you have."

Have others noticed a change in you? Do they call you a

* <http://video.google.com/videoplay?docid=9144522832915746557>

"care giver," "encourager," or "compassionate listener?" Their words may indicate the path God is prompting you to take. Does injustice, oppression, or apathy for a cause or people rouse you? This may be your new mission. Do you feel unqualified, unworthy, or overwhelmed by the challenges of stepping forth to incite change? Ask God's blessing on your work.

The climax of Gideon's quest to strike a blow against God's enemies reads like a military blunder. God commanded this "mighty warrior" to pare down his troops to three hundred: a mere one percent of a thirty thousand man army. But one percent of anything with God by our side is a strategy for success.

"Our protection and prosperity does not come from the sword, or microchip or factories," says Daniels, "but from the hand of God."* Is God deploying me? Is He deploying you? Let's jump from the window and go in the strength He has already supplied.

Discern: Read about Gideon's "jump" in Judges 7:8-25. Why was he successful? What did his success prompt others to do?

_____

_____

_____

_____

_____

_____

_____

_____

Do: Ask at least three people to list your strengths. Tell them to be honest. Lay the lists before God in prayer and ask Him to give you an opportunity to "jump."

_____

_____

_____

_____

_____

_____

_____

_____

_____

_____

_____

_____

If you have received a ministry from the Lord Jesus, you will know that the need is not the same as the call – the need is the opportunity to exercise the call.

Oswald Chambers

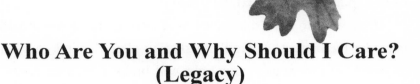

Who Are You and Why Should I Care? (Legacy)

If you spend yourselves in behalf of the hungry and satisfy the needs of the oppressed, then your light will rise in the darkness, and your night will become like the noonday. **Isaiah 58:10 (NIV)**

According to *Publisher's Weekly*, "The power of television and celebrity status was obvious [in 2009]: of the top 15 authors, seven have prominent regular media exposure."* Without a compelling reason, few readers will buy a book from an unknown writer.

We live in a celebrity-driven culture but platform and prominence is not the exclusive domain of the popular and pretty. Mother Teresa didn't have a publicity agent, and she made a name for herself. William Booth was so burdened by the poor and wretched of London's East End that he resigned his position as church minister and founded a mission. Today we know Booth's Salvation Army by the jingle of their bell, not

---

* <http://michaelhyatt.com/how-important-is-an-author%E2%80%99s-media-platform.html>

their blog, web site, or social networking.

Years prior to Booth and Mother Teresa, a simple carpenter went around the countryside touching the untouchables, consoling the widows and eating with drunkards, prostitutes, and the insane. He never published a word, and yet the message of His "platform" changed the world.

If we want to build a legacy, brand, and platform, we should consider the benefits of God's marketing plan: "Spend yourself in behalf of others and your light will break forth like dawn" (honor and success); "healing will appear quickly" (sustaining stamina); "your righteousness will be before you" (no need for a publicity director); "and the glory of the LORD will be your rear guard" (God has your back).

Want to make a name for yourself? Make it your business to help others with the comfort you've received from God.

Discern: Read Isaiah 53. How did God's "root out of dry ground" earn "a portion among the great"?

_____

_____

_____

_____

_____

_____

_____

Do: Write down the names of two people you can comfort with the comfort you've received from God. Then reach out to them with loving words and kind actions.

_____

_____

_____

_____

_____

_____

_____

_____

_____

_____

_____

_____

*Leave the Irreparable Past in His hands,
and step out into the Irresistable Future
with Him.* **Oswald Chambers**

Rise Up and Advance
(Boldness)

If they had been thinking of the country they had
left, they would have had opportunity to return.
Hebrews 11:15 (NIV)

In the winter of 1862, President Lincoln drafted the following message to the head of the Union Army: "My Dear McClellan: If you are not using the army, I should like to borrow it for a short while. Yours respectfully, Abraham Lincoln."

The president's message failed to rouse General George McClellan to action and on January 15, 1862, President Lincoln ordered McClellan to appear before an investigative committee. When asked why he refused to attack, McClellan said that he needed time to prepare the proper routes for retreat. Months later McClellan attacked, but his lethargic movements and Robert E. Lee's unrelenting assaults forced McClellan to abandon his bid to seize the Confederate capital. As expected, McClellan retreated to the safety of Washington.

What does God *expect* of you? When summoned, will you advance or piddle in endless preparation until the opportunity for victory passes? This is the great failure of God's people: Too often we abandon the field of battle before we fully engage the enemy. God doesn't want courageous cowards; He *needs* confident commanders.

God is not surprised when we return to the convenience of our comfortable past. In fact, He offers a "properly prepared" retreat for those who cannot release their past. When God assembled Gideon's army, He told the wavering commander to send home all who were afraid and would not remain alert and vigilant. This is the Commander in Chief we serve.

Too often we attend spiritual retreats but seldom advance beyond our own boastful proclamations of "I'm a follower of Christ"—whatever *that* means. We move in fits and starts and fall back, but that is to be expected if we are not convinced of God's calling. Here are three things you should know about the God you serve:

First, if He has called you to a work, His angels go before you, beside you, and behind you (Psalm 91:11). This bubble of protection will not shield you from an assassin's bullet, but it does enable you to advance in the knowledge that God's hand shadows you.

Second, God's column of fire will give you light by night and warmth by day (Exodus 13:21). His Word, Spirit, and wise counsel—offered from the mouths of godly men and women—will illuminate your path.

Third, He will fight for you (Deuteronomy 1:30). This battle, this job, this opportunity is not yours. It is God's. If you invest your time in prayerful discernment and preparation, you can trust the outcome to Him. You may not see the victory. Many of the heroes of faith did not see their promised land either. But it is better to have fought and died than never tried.

Rise up and advance.

Discern: Read 1 Samuel 14:1-23. What effect did Jonathan's courageous advance have on the rest of the Israelite army? What gave Jonathan the confidence to take that risk?

_____

_____

_____

_____

_____

_____

Do: A double-minded person cannot move forward with confidence, so accept God's leading and act.

_____

_____

_____

_____

_____

_____

_____

_____

_____

_____

_____

_____

_____

_____

_____

Common sense and faith are as different from each other as the natural life is from the spiritual. **Oswald Chambers**

Seeds of Success
(Faith)

And without faith it is impossible to please God, because anyone who comes to him must believe that he exists and that he rewards those who earnestly seek him. **Hebrews 11:6 (NIV)**

A man went out to sow grass. As he scattered the first handful of seed he thought, *This ground is too hard and the sun too hot. What shoots will flourish in this dry soil?* Dropping the rest of the seed back into his pouch, he walked away.

Another man arrived. He too carried a pouch. Kneeling on one knee, he scratched the hard soil. *Dry. Rock hard,* he thought. *This will never work.* Dropping the seed in his pouch, he too walked away. Soon, however, he returned with a small pail of water. Dipping his hand into the bucket and drawing out a handful of water, he moistened the ground until a muddy paste formed. Pressing his thumb into the soil, he placed a seed into the divot he'd created and covered it with soil. He repeated this process until every seed in his pouch had been planted.

For weeks the man returned each day to water his small plot. One day he noticed a green shoot emerging from the soil. The next day he brought more water and began in another part of the field, soaking the soil, massaging the mud, and planting seeds. The man tended his plot each day until he died.

When he awoke in heaven, he found himself resting on a bed of cool grass. From above, a brilliant light warmed his skin. "Grass?" a voice boomed. "This is what you did with your life? You grew grass?"

Startled, the man sat up but saw no one.

"I...I did what I could," the man stammered.

"But grass? With one word I could have carpeted the countryside."

"When I touched the soil it was hard," the man replied. "I know others find it hard to believe in you. They say there is no point, makes no sense. I believed that if I planted seed you would make it grow."

"And if I had not?" asked the voice.

"But you did. When I knelt and rubbed my fingers in the dirt, I sensed your presence, for you formed the earth. As I tended to the seed, I was reminded of how I too would be placed in the ground someday."

"So you had faith that I would care for you in the same way you cared for the seed?"

"Yes. And see? You have. I know this lawn," the man said, running his fingers through the blades of grass.

"Do you expect some great reward for growing grass?"

"I didn't think in those terms. I only did what I could. I scattered seed. Watching you make it grow was reward enough."

A clap of thunder shook the ground. Though the brilliance remained, the man felt rain—not the hard drops he'd known before, but a gentle mist that refreshed him deep within his soul.

"Rise. Let us walk together on your grass," said the voice, "in the cool of the day."

A seed of faith is tiny, but when planted in God's soil, it can spread across acres. Plant kernels of faith today. Work diligently in the field God has provided for you.

Discern: Read Hebrews 11:1-31. What did common sense tell these men and women to do? What did faith tell them to do?

_____

_____

_____

_____

_____

_____

Do: What field has God given you right now? What seeds of faith can you sow in it today?

_____

_____

_____

_____

_____

_____

_____

_____

_____

_____

_____

_____

_____

The supernatural becomes natural to us through the miracle of God.

Oswald Chambers

Have Work Your Way at Bigger King (Commitment)

Therefore since we receive a kingdom which cannot be shaken, let us show gratitude, by which we may offer to God an acceptable service with reverence and awe. **Hebrews 12:28 (NASB)**

In these tough economic times when companies are downsizing, outsourcing, and capsizing, it's hard to find the perfect job. And by "perfect job" I mean one that comes with benefits—like a paycheck. The solution? Go to work for the Bigger King.

The Bigger King can be trusted to keep you employed. The Bigger King has a long track record of employment. He does not discriminate on the basis or race, gender, or marital status, and it has a loyal and growing customer base.

Here are a few reasons you should consider going to work for the Bigger King:

The Bigger King forgives all your sins. If you mess up,

don't worry. The Bigger King will not fire you if you miss your performance goals. He expects perfection but gives you plenty of time to grow into the job. All of eternity, in fact. And if you are struggling in a particular area, His Spirit will give you strength, power, and success.

The Bigger King heals all your diseases. The Bigger King has a great medical plan. If you get sick or injured, don't worry. You're covered. Even if you get deathly ill and can't work, the Bigger King will stay by your bed, encouraging you to get better. He'll remind you that you're loved and missed. He'll affirm that your work is important to Him.

The Bigger King redeems your life from the pit. Think your last job was the pits? You'll love working for the Bigger King. He has a fantastic exchange program. He'll swap all your embarrassing blunders for His glory. Plus, with the Bigger King, you can do any work you choose—even if you don't have any experience in that area. In fact, many of His best workers began as unskilled but eager servants. The Bigger King provides all the training and education you will need to be successful. He places a lot of emphasis on heart, so if you think you can, with Him, you will.

The Bigger King crowns you with love and compassion. The Bigger King not only remembers your birthday, He ordained it. Need a shoulder to cry on? He's there. Want someone to listen while you vent? Call the Bigger King. Do others overlook your work, mistake your intentions, and misjudge your motives? The Bigger King understands exactly how you feel. He too was mistreated, misjudged, and mistaken for a failure. The door is always open to the Bigger King's office. He loves all His workers equally, as if they were His own children.

The Bigger King satisfies your desires with good things. In this company you don't have to "settle" for any old job. The boss man wants you to have a good job and an abundant life. When you sign with the Bigger King, you know your future is in good hands.

With the Bigger King your youth is renewed. The Bigger King Kingdom has a great fitness and wellness program. It's called work. No one gets laid off, takes a "package," or retires.

There you have it: the Bigger King employment package. You salary is non-negotiable. You will be paid according to His riches, not your estimated worth, work experience, education, or perceived importance. Should you decide to go to work for the Bigger King, simply sign this form and say aloud: "Here I am, Lord. Send me."

YES, I AGREE TO WORK FOR THE BIGGER KING, REGARDLESS OF WHAT HE ASKS ME TO DO.

Sign here_____

Discern: Read Luke 14:25-35. According to Jesus, what does the personnel handbook require of the Bigger King's employees?

*all Oswald Chambers quotes are taken from *My Utmost for His Highest* (Grand Rapids: Discovery house publishers, 1935, Copyright renewed 1963 by Oswald Chambers publications Association, Ltd.) with the exception of the quote on page 7, which is taken from *Devotions for a Deeper Life: A Daily Devotional* (Cincinnati: God's Bible school, 1986).

Do: Tell someone that you have signed a contract with the Bigger King. Ask that person to hold you accountable and update that person each week on your work for the Bigger King.